By George Wickey

with illustrations by Claudia Gadotti

30A GAMES

PLAY TOGETHER.

Special thanks to:

Mom (Nancy) & Dad (Regan) for your love, support, and for always believing in me.

Binks for showing me how proud of me you were even in your darkest moment. I'm being strong.

Allison & Jamie for bringing angels into this world.

Genevieve, Mark & Winston for totally getting me, for being there, and for the great meals. Favorite cousins.

Dixie for having a heart of gold, being such a team player, the singing, and the laughter. Meet me somewhere.

AbbyGal and BabyGal for unconditional, exquisite love. I'm honored to be your human. Greet me at the bridge.

Acknowledgments:

Claudia for turning the analog pictures in my mind into the stunning, idyllic artwork in this book.

Lori for being a grammarwitch and for teaching me meter—and then fighting the good fight trying to get me to follow mine.

Allison & Dixie for assorted aesthetic advice.

Hill for helping me put it together right & Nancy for getting it printed and getting it here.

There are countless worthy places and events that are part of the 30A experience that, despite my best efforts, I couldn't make fit in this book.

I'm sorry!

Copyright © 2014 by George Wickey

No part of this book may be used or reproduced in any form or manner whatsoever without written permission from the author.

All rights reserved. Published by 30A Games, LLC

www.30agames.com

Production Date: March 2014

Plant & Location: Printed by Everbest Printing (Guangzhou, China), Co. Ltd

Job / Batch # 114794.3

Library of Congress Cataloging-in-Publication Data

Wickey, George

The 30A Book, by George Wickey; illustrated by Claudia Gadotti. --- 1st ed.

p. cm.

ISBN 978-0-9916324-3-5

For Cal, Cam and Kate ...

We made the drive down Highway 331.
It took a long time; we found ways to have fun.

We sang songs and played a game with license plates
Trying hard to find cars from all 50 states!

"Are we almost there yet?" It seemed so far out of reach
That we thought we would never arrive at the beach.

Then it got very quiet, there wasn't a peep;
Baby Sister and I had just fallen asleep.

But, in what seemed like minutes, when we woke from our nap,
It was time for a movie, some juice and a snack. When—

"We're crossing the bridge!" High up over the bay,

Then we make our last turn,
and we're on 30A!

You should trust me on this, for what it is worth:
30A just might be the best place on this earth.

It has beautiful beaches, the Gulf is so clear,
And it stays nice and warm nearly all of the year.

The water is emerald; the sand sugary white,
And there's so much to do every day, every night.

Emerald water, sugary white sand ...

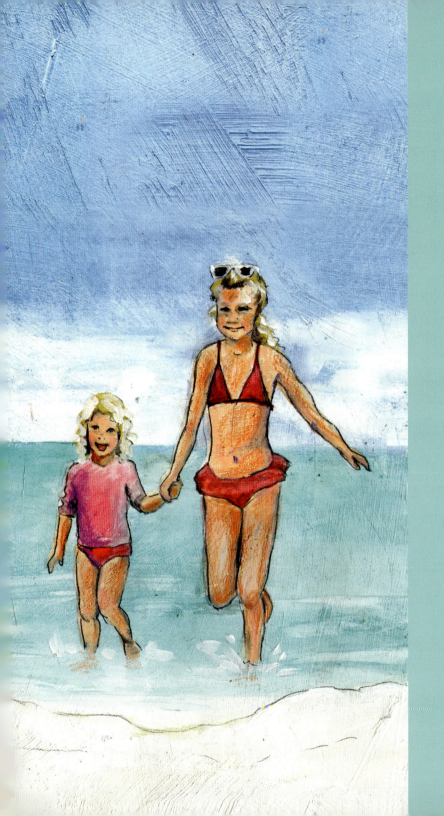

You can play in the surf
and bathe in the sun,

Sculpt castles of sand; why,
you've only begun!

Rent a four-wheel surrey and together you'll ride!

Catch crabs with a net and see movies outside.

Sleep in a cottage on bunks stacked in 3's,
Romp through playgrounds, catch fish, fly a kite, and climb trees.

Tour state parks, ride a YOLO Board, watch dolphins at play!
Board games on the porch pass the whole lazy day.

Visit Seaside, WaterColor, Rosemary, and Alys Beach.

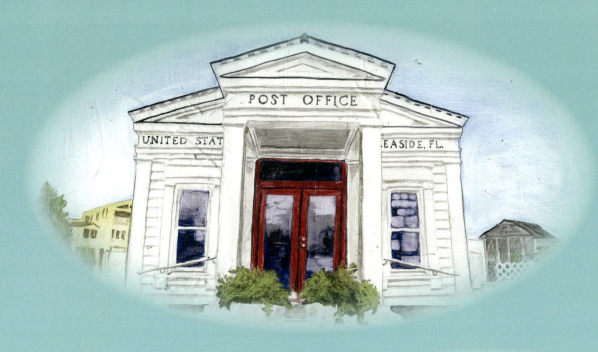

Which one is my favorite? I'd have to say each.

Which is your favorite?

But don't forget Grayton with "nice dogs, friendly folks" too, where we drive out for sunset to enjoy the grayt view.

Past the big coastal dune lake, behind dunes and tall trees…

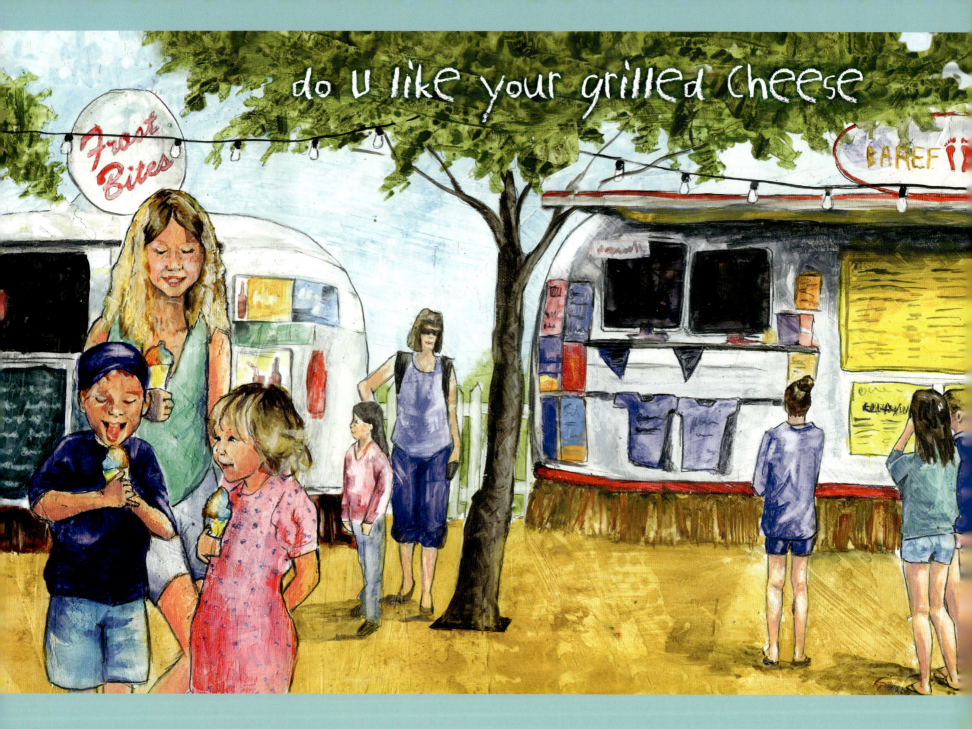

Old silver trailers sell shaved ice and grilled cheese.

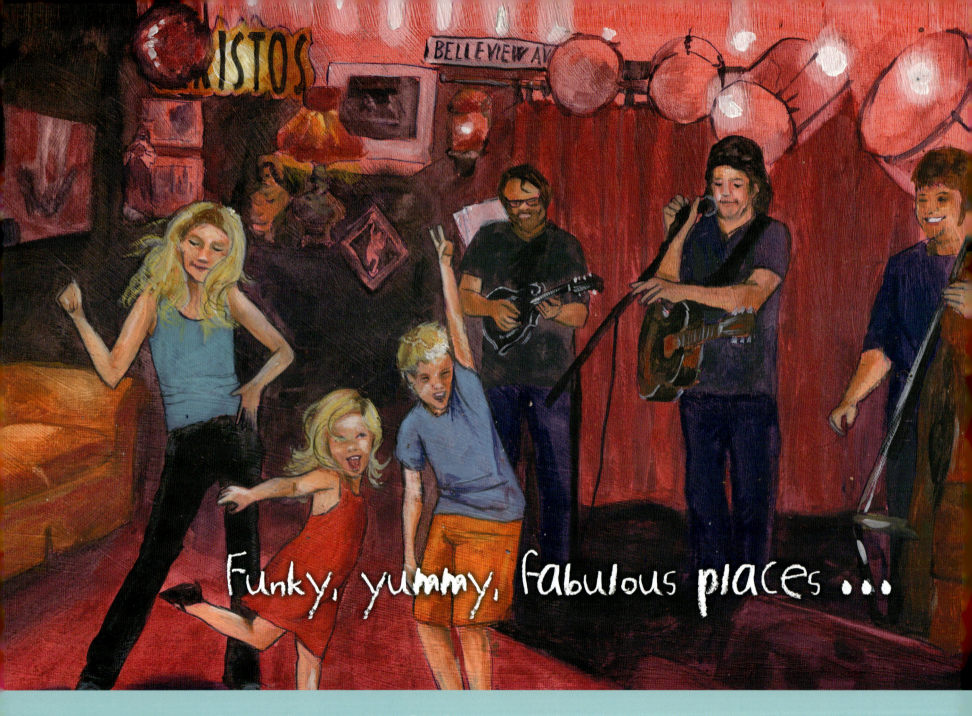

There's live music, funky art, and yummy places too,
Like Donut Hole, Red Bar, and Stinky's Fish Camp—to name a few.

There's Fired Up to paint pottery and Gigi's for fabulous fashions and toys,
There's Duckies Shop of Fun and Little Red for girls and boys.

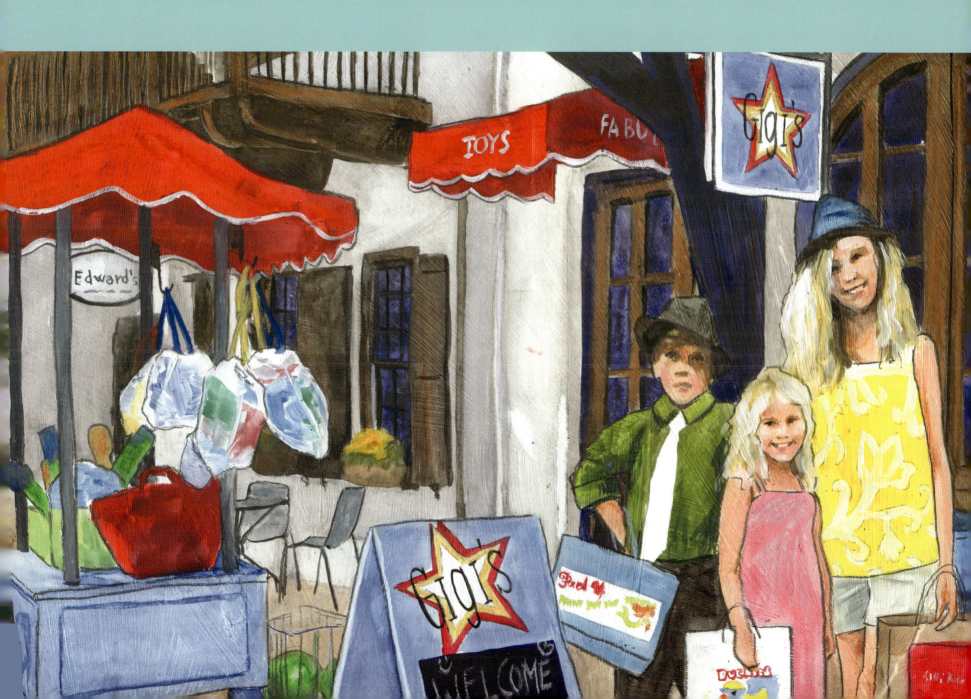

There's a store for books called Sundog with old records in the back,

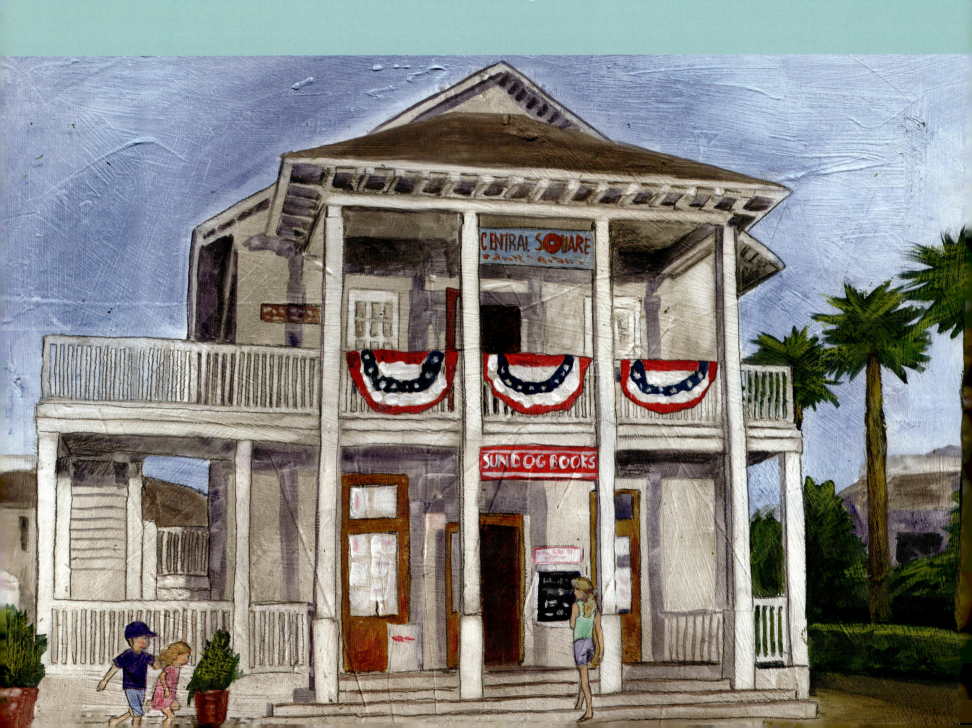

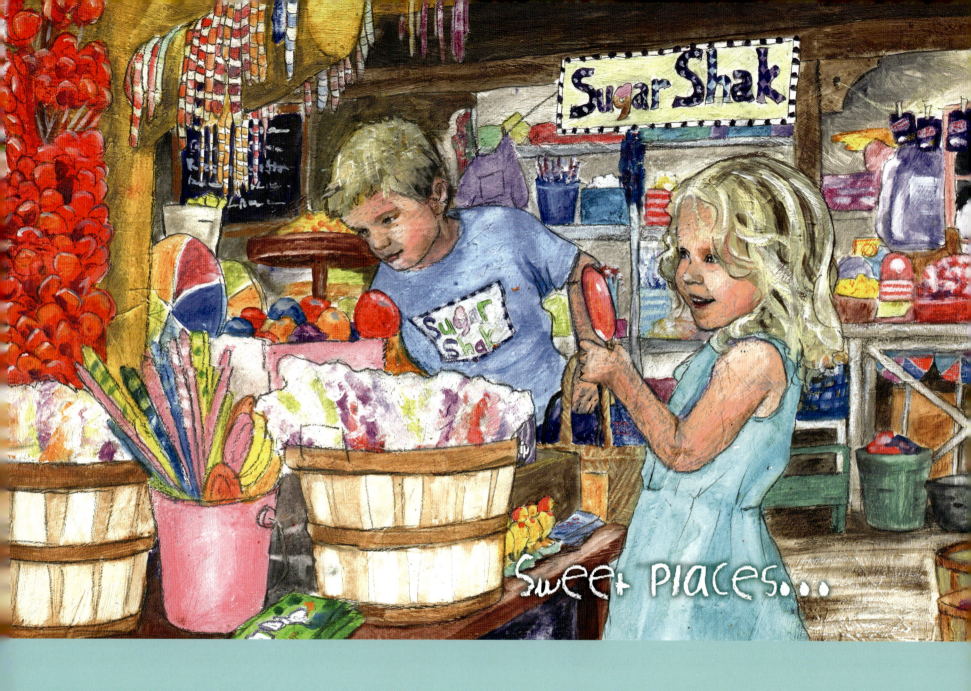

For ice cream cones or candy, there's a place called Sugar Shak.

When you're having such fun, the time flies, grown-ups say,
But it's hard to believe that this is our last day.

So we'll play at the beach; it would only be right,
Then toast s'mores by a bonfire to close out the night.

Now our bags are all packed, almost ready to go
Back to school, home, and friends, and the places we know.

Perhaps someday we'll be locals, so lucky to live here...
But now, goodbye 30A! We will see you next year!